IMAGES OF WAR

HEYDRICH

THE BUTCHER OF PRAGUE

RARE PHOTOGRAPHS FROM WARTIME ARCHIVES

Ian Baxter

Pen & Sword
MILITARY

First published in Great Britain in 2022 by
PEN & SWORD MILITARY
an imprint of Pen & Sword Books Ltd
Yorkshire – Philadelphia

ISBN 978-1-39909-756-7

A CIP catalogue record for this book is available from the British Library.

Typeset by Concept, Huddersfield, West Yorkshire, HD4 5JL.
Printed and bound in England by CPI Group (UK) Ltd, Croydon CR0 4YY.

MIX
Paper from responsible sources
FSC® C013604

Pen & Sword Books Limited incorporates the imprints of Atlas, Archaeology, Aviation, Discovery, Family History, Fiction, History, Maritime, Military, Military Classics, Politics, Select, Transport, True Crime, Air World, Frontline Publishing, Leo Cooper, Remember When, Seaforth Publishing, The Praetorian Press, Wharncliffe Local History, Wharncliffe Transport, Wharncliffe True Crime and White Owl.

For a complete list of Pen & Sword titles please contact
PEN & SWORD BOOKS LTD
47 Church Street, Barnsley, South Yorkshire, S70 2AS, England
E-mail: enquiries@pen-and-sword.co.uk
Website: www.pen-and-sword.co.uk
or
PEN & SWORD BOOKS
1950 Lawrence Rd, Havertown, PA 19083, USA
E-mail: uspen-and-sword@casematepublishers.com
Website: www.penandswordbooks.com

Contents

About the Author

Ian Baxter is a military historian who specialises in German twentieth-century military history. He has written more than fifty books including *Poland – The Eighteen Day Victory March, Panzers In North Africa, The Ardennes Offensive, The Western Campaign, The 12th SS Panzer-Division Hitlerjugend, The Waffen-SS on the Western Front, The Waffen-SS on the Eastern Front, The Red Army at Stalingrad, Elite German Forces of World War II, Armoured Warfare, German Tanks of War, Blitzkrieg, Panzer-Divisions at War, Hitler's Panzers, German Armoured Vehicles of World War Two, Last Two Years of the Waffen-SS at War, German Soldier Uniforms and Insignia, German Guns of the Third Reich, Defeat to Retreat: The Last Years of the German Army At War 1943–45, Operation Bagration – the Destruction of Army Group Centre, German Guns of the Third Reich, Rommel and the Afrika Korps, U-Boat War,* and most recently *The Sixth Army and the Road to Stalingrad.* He has written over a hundred articles including 'Last days of Hitler', 'Wolf's Lair', 'The Story of the V1 and V2 Rocket Programme', 'Secret Aircraft of World War Two', 'Rommel at Tobruk', 'Hitler's War With his Generals', 'Secret British Plans to Assassinate Hitler', 'The SS at Arnhem', 'Hitlerjugend', 'Battle of Caen 1944', 'Gebirgsjäger at War', 'Panzer Crews', 'Hitlerjugend Guerrillas', 'Last Battles in the East', 'The Battle of Berlin', and many more. He has also reviewed numerous military studies for publication, supplied thousands of photographs and important documents to various publishers and film production companies worldwide, and lectures to various schools, colleges and universities throughout the United Kingdom and the Republic of Ireland.

Foreword

The reign of *SS-Obergruppenführer* Reinhard Heydrich in Bohemia and Moravia will forever remain in the history of the Second World War as a period of terror, immense brutality and mass killings of Czech citizens. However, it was also a time of great solidarity and heroism among the Czech people in spite of the deaths of thousands of innocent men, women and children. The population lived in daily fear for themselves and their loved ones, but despite the constant trepidation, resistance to Nazism was strong in Czechoslovakia.

One of the most powerful Nazis of the Third Reich, Reinhard Heydrich, who became protector of Bohemia and Moravia in September 1941, soon earned the nickname of 'the executioner of the Czech nation' and 'the Butcher of Prague'.

However, after only eight months in office, Heydrich would be attacked in Prague on 27 May 1942 by two Czech paratroopers, Jozef Gabčík and Jan Kubiš. Heydrich would later die from his injuries and as a result there were brutal consequences for the Czech citizens and terrible reprisals would follow.

This book is the story of Reinhard Heydrich's rise to power. He became the darkest figure within the Nazi regime and would become known by his Führer as the man with the iron heart.

Michal Výborný
Prague

Introduction

Reinhard Heydrich was a high-ranking SS and police official and a main architect of the Holocaust. He was chief of the Reich Main Security Office and became deputy and acting Reich Protector of Bohemia and Moravia.

This book, with rare and previously unpublished photographs together with in-depth captions and text, chronicles the story of Heydrich, who later became known as the Butcher of Prague for suppressing Czech culture and deporting and executing members of the Czech Resistance. Brutal and callous, he was directly responsible for the *Einsatzgruppen*, the special task forces that travelled in the wake of the German armies, and murdered more than 2 million people by mass shooting and gassing, including 1.3 million Jews. He also chaired the January 1942 Wannsee Conference which formalized plans for the 'Final Solution to the Jewish Question'.

However, in May 1942 Heydrich was critically wounded in Prague as a result of Operation ANTHROPOID. Following his assassination, the Nazi State declared a State Funeral in Prague and then another in Berlin. This book reveals unique photos of the funeral held at Hitler's Reich Chancellery.

With Heydrich dead, the Czech people suffered huge reprisals which saw the villages of Lidice and Ležáky razed to the ground and the inhabitants either sent to concentration camps or executed.

Chapter One

Early Years

Reinhard Heydrich is regarded as one of the darkest figures in the Nazi hierarchy. He joined the Nazi Party in June 1931 and by August that same year had joined the realms of the SS. During this time Heinrich Himmler, leader of the SS, began setting up a counter-intelligence section of the SS and met Heydrich for an informal meeting at a railway station in Eberstein. Himmler was so impressed with Heydrich's ideas that he hired him straight away.

Heydrich began his role as chief of the new 'Ic Service' (Intelligence Service) from the Nazi Party head office in Munich called the Brown House. Within weeks of taking the job he had formed a large network of spies and informers. By December Himmler had promoted him to the rank of *SS-Sturmbannführer*.

In mid-1932 Himmler appointed Heydrich as chief of the renamed security service: *Sicherheitsdienst* (Security Service or SD). Consequently, Heydrich's power grew over the next couple of years, turning a small counter-intelligence department into an efficient machine of fear and intimidation.

By June 1934 Heydrich had become head of the Gestapo, which he used as an instrument of terror against his opponents. Over the next couple of years the Gestapo earned its infamous reputation with its policemen using torture and violence as their key to interrogation.

In June 1936 Hitler decreed the unification of all police forces in Germany and named Himmler as Chief of German Police. With this appointment Himmler and his deputy Heydrich became the most powerful and feared men in Germany. Himmler immediately restructured and organized the police, with Heydrich having the security agencies separated into two groups comprising the *Ordnungspolizei* (Order Police or *Orpo*), consisting of the national uniformed police and the municipal police plus the Security Police. The Security Police was made up of the combined forces of the Gestapo and the *Kriminalpolizei* (Criminal Police or *Kripo*).

With Heydrich now at the zenith of his power he became the chief enforcer of Nazi terror inside Germany. He was able to widen his network of fear to persecute more and more groups including unionists, intellectuals, liberal priests, Seventh-Day Adventists, sexual minorities, gypsies and, the most reviled people in his eyes, the Jews.

Following the Anschluss in Austria in March 1938, under the direction of the SS Heydrich then formed one of the most fearsome of all the groups under his control known as the *Einsatzgruppen* (deployment forces or task forces). They were created from an ad hoc *Einsatzkommando* and were responsible for securing government buildings and documents. Originally these *Einsatzkommandos* were part of the *Sicherheitspolizei* (Security Police or *SiPo*).

Later that year, when the Sudetenland was assigned to Germany between 1 and 10 October 1938, Heydrich ordered two units of the *Einsatzgruppen* to be moved to the region and given the task of removing all government papers and police documents. They were also ordered to surround and raid the government buildings and detain and question senior civil servants, which included the arrest of more than 10,000 Czech communists and German citizens.

During this time Heydrich was also tasked to deport Jews out of Germany, during which operation he used every method possible, including a nationwide pogrom, to terrify Jews into leaving. His actions included what later became known as 'the Night of Broken Glass' (*Kristallnacht*) on 9/10 November 1938. More than 1,000 synagogues and 7,000 Jewish businesses had been attacked. More than 90 people had been murdered and 30,000 Jews were arrested and sent to concentration camps. To further intimidate the Jewish people, it was Heydrich who proposed that Jews should be forced to wear a signifying mark such as a yellow star on their clothes, but Hitler refused at this point.

Over the coming months while the Jews were continually mistreated and intimidated, the German war machine prepared itself for war against Poland. Although Heydrich had immense powers within the Nazi State at this time, his purview was still initially limited to internal policing. However, as preparations against Poland were being made, his power would swiftly expand.

A postcard showing a swastika flag flying over the Brown House, the Nazi Party headquarters in Munich.

Reinhard Heydrich handing a piece of paper to Alfred Naujocks in April 1934 from his desk at his Brown House headquarters in Munich. Naujocks was initially a low-ranking driver for the *Sicherheitsdienst* SD-Regional Command East, Berlin in 1934, but Heydrich soon entrusted him with special assignments such as murder.

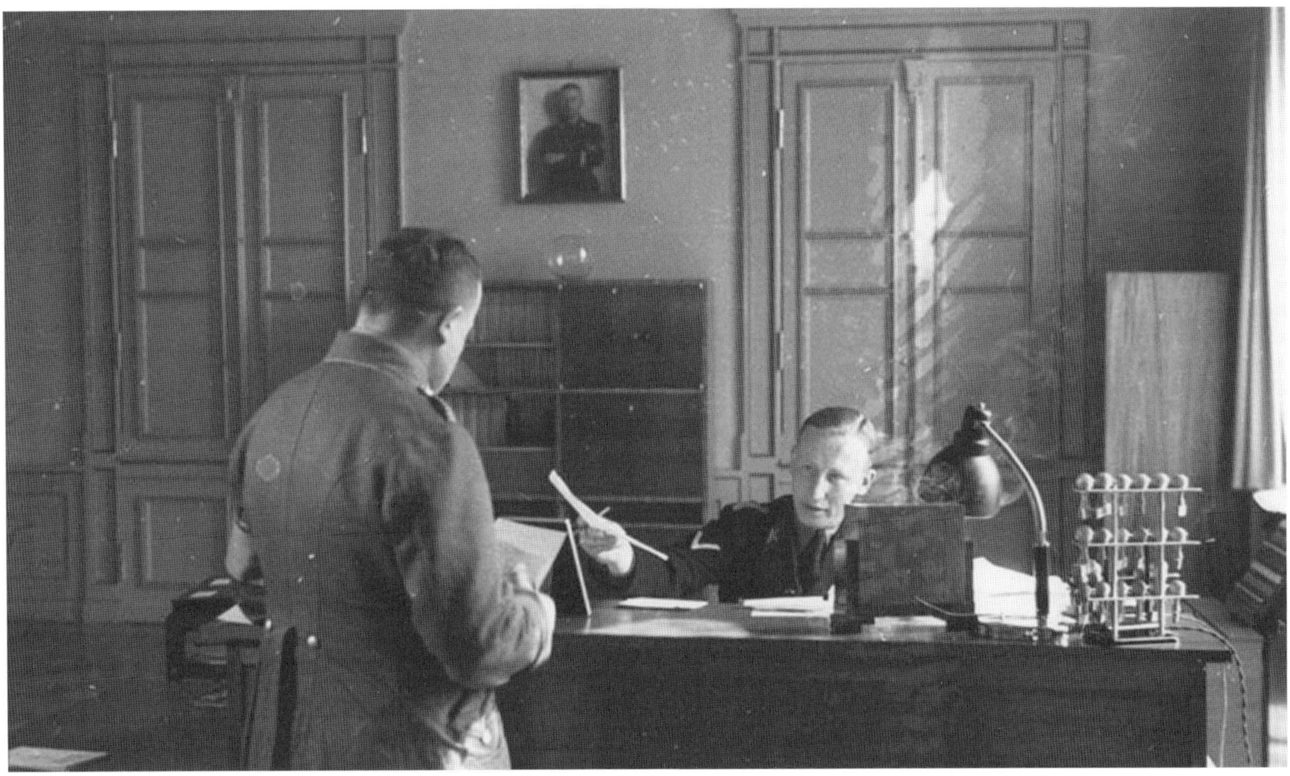

Two photographs showing *SS-Brigadeführer* Heydrich working at his desk from his Brown House headquarters in Berlin in 1934. During this period he was head of the Bavarian Police and chief of the SD.

A photograph of the *Geheimes Staatspolizeihauptamt*, or Gestapo headquarters, which was at 8 Prinz Albrecht Street in Berlin. On 22 April 1934 Heydrich was appointed head of the Gestapo by Himmler. Both men employed young and highly-educated officers into the Gestapo, which had a wide variety of academic fields. Heydrich in particular looked for candidates that were hard-working, efficient and prepared to carry the Nazi state forward through the persecution of their political opponents. As a result, the Gestapo immediately became an instrument of terror under SS control.

A portrait photograph of Heydrich as commander of the Gestapo. As soon as Heydrich was appointed to his new position he began building the Gestapo into an instrument of fear. Under his complete control he had the authority to arrest citizens on suspicion that they might commit a crime, and the definition of a crime was at his discretion.

(**Right**) Heydrich sitting on some steps with his sword following a memorial service. In 1935 Himmler began developing the concept of a new religion known as the Germanic religion. He wanted all SS members to leave the church. In early 1936, Heydrich left the Catholic Church in favour of the *Gottglaubig* movement.

(**Below**) Himmler with Heydrich visits the preparations for the memorial service of Reich President Paul von Hindenburg. This was known as the Tannenberg Memorial, or *Tannenberg-Nationaldenkmal*, and was a monument to the German soldiers of the Battle of Tannenberg, the First Battle of the Masurian Lakes and the medieval Battle of Tannenberg in 1410. The victorious German commander General Field Marshal von Hindenburg, who became a national hero, was later interred there on site. A memorial service was held in honour of him and the battle, of which the SS played a big part in marking.

(**Opposite, above**) Heydrich is in the centre of a group of German police officials during a visit to the tomb of the unknown soldier.

(**Opposite, below**) Himmler and Heydrich are seen here climbing some steps. By mid-June 1936, all police forces throughout Germany were united and Himmler was made Chief of German Police. With this appointment by Hitler, Himmler and his deputy Heydrich became two of the most powerful men in the internal administration of the Reich.

Heydrich can be seen to the left of Himmler with an Italian fascist delegation.

Heydrich and other SS officers with their wives in 1937.

Leaving his hotel with Heydrich in Vienna, both Himmler and Heydrich can be seen here in front of the Hotel Metropol in Vienna after the *Anschluss* of Austria on 12 March 1938.

Himmler can be seen here attending a swearing ceremony of the Austrian Police in March 1938 on Heldenplatz in Vienna. Heydrich can just be seen within the entourage walking behind the *Reichsführer*. With the unification of Germany and Austria, Himmler and Heydrich quickly ordered the suppression of all opposition. In fact, even before the first German soldier crossed the border, both men began arresting prominent representatives of those they regarded would be hostile to the Reich.

A still taken from a film showing Hitler, Himmler and Heydrich together during a ceremony.

Arthur Seyss-Inquart, Adolf Hitler, Heinrich Himmler and Heydrich in Vienna in March 1938. In February 1938, Seyss-Inquart was appointed Austrian Minister of the Interior by Schuschnigg after Hitler had threatened Schuschnigg with military actions against Austria in the event of non-compliance. Just weeks later Seyss-Inquart drafted the legislative act reducing Austria to a province of Germany and signed it into law on 13 March.

Himmler and Heydrich can be seen here climbing some steps at Prague Castle. By the late 1930s Heydrich was at the peak of his power and became the chief enforcer of Nazi terror inside Germany. With his vast chain of contacts and police network he was able to widen his net of fear and persecute more and more groups, all of which were in his mind 'hostile elements of the Reich'.

At a luncheon *SS-Obergruppenführer* Werner Best is seen with a representative of the Hungarian police in Berlin in February 1939. Heydrich made Best head of Amt I (Department I) of the RSHA: Administration and Legal. It was a department that dealt with the legal and personnel issues/matters of the SS and security police. Both Heydrich and Himmler relied on Best to develop and explain legally the activities against enemies of the state and in relation to the Nazi Jewish policy.

Chapter Two

Tannenberg

As a pretext for attacking Poland in September 1939, Hitler asked Himmler, Heydrich and Heinrich Müller to mastermind a plan known as Operation HIMMLER. The plan involved a fake attack on the German radio station at Gleiwitz on 31 August 1939. It was Heydrich that had gone out to the Polish border and toured the area with some of his staff and then concocted the plan. He told his boss, Himmler, that in order to stage the attack, concentration camp prisoners would be dressed in Polish army uniforms. They would then be given lethal injections in order to prove that these 'soldiers' had attacked the German frontier, thereby giving the excuse that Poland had launched an initial attack against Germany.

When the German invasion was launched on 1 September 1939, this undercover operation was one of several instigated by a special *Abwehr* (Military Intelligence Service) army and Security Service volunteer unit.

The war against Poland was swift, and during the invasion Heydrich and Himmler began formulating plans and ideas of how they were going to deal with the country racially. Both men shared a view of the identity of the enemies of the German race and the measures to be taken against them. Like Himmler, Heydrich believed that the destruction of its opponents would be sufficient to guarantee the security and survival of the German nation.

As a result, Himmler instructed Heydrich to form his *Einsatzgruppen* units to travel in the wake of the German armies through Poland. On 21 September 1939, Heydrich sent out a teleprinter message on the 'Jewish question in the occupied territory' to the chiefs of all *Einsatzgruppen* with implicit orders to round up all the Jewish people in Poland with the intention of placing them into holding areas for ghettos. However, in reality, Heydrich's plans were more barbaric than just rounding up those they regarded as hostile to the Reich. In a series of meetings he had outlined that the mission of the *Einsatzgruppen* through Poland would be to kill members of the Polish leadership. This would include the intelligentsia, teachers, the clergy and the nobility. Using dossiers collected by the SD, lists were drawn up of people to be killed in Poland. Part of this list included members of Polish society, Jews, prostitutes, Romani people and the mentally ill. For this action the *Einsatzgruppen*, along with auxiliary personnel, SS and police units, were tasked not with employing their military capabilities but instead with terrorizing the civilian population through acts that included hunting down straggling Polish soldiers, confiscating livestock and agricultural produce, and torturing and murdering large numbers of Polish political leaders, businessmen, priests, intellectuals and Jews.

For these operations in Poland Heydrich selected none other than his deputy, *SS-Obergruppenführer* Werner Best, who was a local Nazi with strong ideological views. Together they formulated their plans, giving the *Einsatzgruppen* operations the cover name TANNENBERG, thought to be named after Germany's greatest single victory of the First World War.

As soon as Heydrich's *Einsatzgruppen* were released into the rear areas, the units quickly gained a reputation, and in a matter of days they began eradicating the Poles by means of torturing and killing. By the end of the campaign in Poland, it was estimated that some 531 towns and villages had been burned, during which events there were many incidents of plunder, banditry and murder.

Following Operation TANNENBERG, Heydrich ordered a second phase of the *Unternehmen* (Operation) to commence. Once again, this included a widespread cleansing action in Poland, utilizing members of the *Einsatzgruppen*. In Pomerania alone, a period of unrestrained terror continued with some 40,000 Poles, including children, being killed before the end of 1939. Both Himmler and Heydrich were determined to kill as many people as possible in order for the transition of the so-called 'ghettoization' of the Jews to be made easier. On 29 November 1939 Heydrich issued an instruction about the 'Evacuation of New Eastern Provinces', outlining the deportation by railway to detention centres, concentration camps and ghettos.

Following the destruction of Poland, Himmler outlined to Heydrich that he was determined this newly-conquered country would be part of his ideological and racial dream. He was going to make sure that Poland would be dismembered, subdivided and repopulated in such a way that it would never be able to rise against Germany again. For the inhabitants of Poland, however, they were compelled to live out their lives according to Himmler's plans for the next five years, in which they were to observe helplessly as the country was racially destroyed. As for Heydrich, he would be given powers to undertake mass murder of those that remained incarcerated inside the doomed country.

What followed was a period of more or less unchecked terror in Poland, particularly in the incorporated areas. Those that were not incorporated comprised a population of some 11 million termed the 'General Government'. This large unincorporated area was deemed the dumping ground for all undesirables and those deemed enemies of the State. It was here that the first deportations of Poles and Jews were sent and where the first ghettos would be erected. The Germans saw the ghettos purely as a provisional measure to control and segregate Jews while the Nazi leadership in Berlin deliberated on their fate for their ultimate removal.

A posed photograph of Heydrich. By the summer of 1939, the Nazis required a pretext for attacking Poland. Hitler asked Himmler, Heydrich and Heinrich Müller to mastermind a plan known as Operation HIMMLER. The plan would involve a fake attack on the German radio station at Gleiwitz.

A photograph of the German radio station at Gleiwitz. *SS-Sturmbannführer* Alfred Naujocks organized a plan under direct orders from Heydrich and Müller, chief of the Gestapo, to stage an incident to prove that Poland started the war first. On the night of 31 August 1939, a small group of German operatives dressed in Polish uniforms and led by Naujocks seized the Gleiwitz station and broadcast a short anti-German message in Polish. The operation was code-named *Grossmutter gestorben* ('Grandmother died'). On 1 September, the day following the Gleiwitz attack, Germany launched the invasion of Poland under the pretext of the 'Polish saboteurs' at Gleiwitz.

Two photographs depicting the German invasion of Poland. On the morning of 1 September 1939 the Wehrmacht launched their attack against a bewildered Polish force. What would follow under Heydrich's orders was widespread murder of those they considered 'hostile elements of the Reich'.

An *Ordnungspolizei* police street check in Kraków. The *Ordnungspolizei* encompassed virtually all of Nazi Germany's law enforcement and emergency response organizations. In Poland they typically rounded up Jews and interrogated them, working closely with the SS and Heydrich's notorious *Einsatzgruppen*. They often handed over Jews and anyone they suspected of being unreceptive to the German regime.

Priests have been rounded up here in a Polish square and it is almost certain that they will be murdered by the *Einsatzgruppen*. In a series of meetings held in August 1939, Heydrich had outlined that the mission of the *Einsatzgruppen* would be to kill members of the Polish leadership. This would include the intelligentsia, teachers, the clergy and the nobility. As Hitler outlined, '… there must be no Polish leaders; where Polish leaders exist they must be killed, however harsh that sounds.' Using dossiers collected by the SD, lists were drawn up of people to be killed in Poland. Part of this list included members of Polish society, Jews, prostitutes, Romani people and the mentally ill.

Thousands of Polish refugees crammed the roads during the German invasion of Poland, often fleeing for their lives or from persecution. In some cases they would come up against advancing *Einsatzgruppen* units and were killed.

Jewish gentlemen are being rounded up by a Wehrmacht security unit and their fate can only be imagined.

Here a Wehrmacht security unit has entered a Polish town and the local folk are being collected. It is almost certain that they are being led away to be murdered.

SS personnel lead blindfolded Polish prisoners to an execution site near Warsaw. *(USHMM)*

SS personnel converse during operations in Poland. Both SS and police units were tasked not only with employing their military capabilities on the battlefields of Poland, but terrorizing the civilian population through acts that included hunting down straggling Polish soldiers, confiscating livestock and agricultural produce, and torturing and murdering large numbers of Polish political leaders, businessmen, priests, intellectuals and Jews.

A typical photograph of murder during the invasion of Poland. Here a group of Poles have been rounded up under orders of an *Ordnungspolizei* unit. Note a Wehrmacht soldier assisting in digging the grave. Note that they are standing inside their own grave, which probably suggests that they were forced to dig it first before being killed.

An *Einsatzgruppen* soldier stands next to a group of Polish people that he has just murdered. Heydrich told his *Einsatzgruppen* commanders that Poland was a 'cleansing and security measure', and their active duty in Poland would give the villages and towns through which it passed a fitting introduction to the character of German rule. The *Einsatzgruppen* operation, he said, had been given the cover name TANNENBERG.

A photograph showing the appalling mass murder of Polish townsmen in western Poland. Heydrich made every commander aware that each *Einsatzkommando* should advance through the Polish heartlands conducting house searches, securing areas from insurgents and arresting and summarily dealing with anyone they deemed to be 'suspicious elements' including Polish civilians and Jews. This order also included the mentally ill and the disabled plus patients recuperating inside hospitals or convalescing at home from various ailments or operations.

Hitler, Himmler and Heydrich can be seen here conversing in the Hradčany Castle in Prague, 1939. Following on from Operation TANNENBERG, Heydrich launched the second phase of the *Unternehmen*. This once again included a widespread cleansing action in Poland, utilizing members of the *Einsatzgruppen*. In Pomerania alone, a period of unrestrained terror continued with some 40,000 Poles, including children, being killed before the end of 1939.

Franz Josef Huber, Arthur Nebe, Himmler, Heydrich and Heinrich Müller are seen here around a table planning the investigation of the bomb assassination attempt on Hitler in Munich, 1939. Following investigations, it was found that carpenter Georg Elser had decided to kill Hitler at the Munich Bürgerbräukeller on 8 November, which was a ceremony marking the anniversary of the Führer's attempted putsch in 1923. Elser had gained access to the venue and found that the hall was not guarded. He systematically prepared his assassination attempt, constructing a detonator mechanism and obtaining explosives. Following the failed attempt, Elser was quickly arrested and after several days of interrogations in Munich, he confessed to the attempted assassination. Heydrich initially thought that Elser was an instrument of the British secret service. He was incarcerated in solitary confinement and would be murdered in Dachau concentration camp on 9 April 1945.

A portrait photograph of Heydrich taken in 1940. With the success of Heydrich's TANNENBERG operations, by 1940 large areas of Poland were incorporated into the Reich. The final task of the *Einsatzgruppen* was to round up the remaining Jews and concentrate them in the growing ghetto system that was being erected within major cities and towns. In order to alleviate some of the burden of 'dumping' them in the already overcrowded ghettos, they drove tens of thousands of men, women and children, with the support of the police and Wehrmacht, eastwards into Soviet-controlled territory.

Himmler can be seen here conferring with Hermann Göring. Standing behind the *Reichsführer* is Heydrich. It was on 31 July 1941 that Göring, writing under instructions from Hitler, ordered Heydrich 'to submit to me as soon as possible a general plan of the administrative material and financial measures necessary for carrying out the desired final solution of the Jewish question.' Göring had already outlined preparations for the 'final solution', which had been drawn up on 24 January 1939. Now with Poland conquered and the Soviet Union under attack, he made it clear that the programme of what would become mass systematic extermination was to encompass 'all the territories of Europe under German occupation'. Heydrich would play a fundamental part in its planning.

Chapter Three

Genocide

During the first cold months of 1940, the Polish 'General Government' continued absorbing thousands of homeless and penniless people into an area that was already overpopulated. In their place came thousands of ethnic Germans moving into the newly-incorporated territories, all of which had to be provided with suitable housing. The scale of the relocation was enormous and chaotic.

By February the immense problems of simultaneously attempting to relocate Poles, Jews and the ethnic Germans had become such an administrative nightmare that it was agreed that all Jews should be forced to live in ghettos. This would not only relieve the burden of the resettlement programme, but it was a way of temporarily getting rid of the growing Jewish problem. The Nazis hated and feared the Jews, and to isolate them in ghettos was deemed immediately practicable for it was believed that Eastern Jews in particular were carriers of diseases and needed to be isolated.

While plans were put into practice creating ghettos, the SS asserted its need to pursue harsh policies in order to deal with the threat of subversion by Polish nationalists and Jewish Bolshevists in the newly-incorporated territories. By early 1940 the situation in various detention centres and concentration camps was untenable due to the new policies of arresting and detaining enemies of the State. News had circulated through SS channels that government officials were demanding immediate action in the expansion of the concentration camp system through its newly-conquered territory of Poland. The German authorities quickly established various camps in Poland where the inmates could be incarcerated and set to work as stone-breakers and construction workers. It was envisaged that these Poles would remain as a slave labour force, and it was therefore deemed necessary to erect these so-called 'quarantine camps' in order to subdue the local population.

Initially it had been proposed that the 'quarantine camps' were to hold the prisoners until they were sent to the various other concentration camps in the Reich. However, it soon became apparent that this purpose was totally impracticable, so it was approved that these camps were to function as a permanent prison for all those that were unfortunate enough to have been sent there.

Throughout 1940 the SS concentration camp system began to expand. Yet, despite this overall vision, the Jews still posed a major problem to any future plans. By

1940 they were being sent to ghettos throughout Poland and contained there, while many others were sent directly to labour and concentration camps.

When the Germans unleashed their attack against the Soviet Union on 22 June 1941, the Jewish problem escalated further. For the Nazi empire the prospect of a war against Russia entailed a transition from one policy of murder to another. This in effect brought about the most radical ideas imaginable in the eyes of Himmler and Heydrich. To deal with the Jews in Russia Heydrich once again utilized his *Einsatzgruppen*, and what followed through the Soviet heartlands was a bloodbath against the Jewish population with widespread murder and executions.

However, in spite of the mass killings, the method of shooting was not regarded as practical as it was not only time-consuming but would have detrimental effects on the troops and, most importantly, would lower morale. Himmler told Heydrich that he wanted a more effective method of killing such as explosives or gas.

The use of gas was not a new method used by the Nazi State. In fact a special department known as T4 had organized the 'Euthanasia Programme', which had first used gassing installations in Germany to kill the insane and incurably ill.

Dr Albert Widmann of the RSHA's Criminal Technical Institute described a new method of using gas vans for mass murder:

> After only a brief period, the commandos of the *Einsatzgruppen* got into considerable difficulties. The members of the *Einsatz* and special commandos, some of whom were themselves fathers, were in the long run not up to the mental strain caused by the mass shootings, particularly when women and children were involved. There were disputes, refusals to obey orders and drunken orgies, but also serious psychological illness. Himmler, who was at first not aware of the situation, was looking for a way of reducing the nervous psychological strain on the men involved in the shooting. Thus, in discussions with Heydrich and other leading figures, the plan emerged of utilizing gas vans for this purpose, which were to be used for the liquidation of women and children in particular ... In September or October 1941, the head of Department IID in the RSHA, *SS-Obersturmbannführer* Rauff, was ordered by Heydrich to build gas vans.

Although many thousands of Jews and Russians were captured and herded into the new gas vans and murdered, Heydrich was given numerous reports that they were not very popular with the SS since they were deemed more unpleasant to operate than the mass executions by shooting. However, Heydrich knew they were to remain the preferred method of liquidation until genocide could be properly perfected in the growing concentration camp system.

During the summer of 1941 Heydrich was continually kept busy with both home and foreign affairs. His brutal nature and success in the implementation of his murder squads and T4 programme led to him being appointed Deputy Reich Protector of the Protectorate of Bohemia and Moravia on 27 September. This was the area of Czechoslovakia that was incorporated into the Reich on 15 March 1939, and Heydrich assumed control of the territory. He was to enforce policy, fight resistance to the Nazi regime and maintain and increase armaments production. As soon as he was appointed to his new role, Heydrich told his aides: 'We will Germanize the Czech vermin.' In his mind's eye he looked upon the Czech people with contempt and outlined that those who could not be Germanized were to die.

Within days of him taking control of Bohemia and Moravia, he began waging an unprecedented reign of terror against the population, terrorizing them and proclaiming martial law. Within five days of his arrival in Prague he had 142 members of the Resistance executed and posters of them were plastered across the occupied country as a warning to others. Over the coming weeks and months, according to Heydrich's staff, the Deputy Reich Protector had between 4,000 and 5,000 people arrested, with many of them executed or sent to concentration camps to be killed. Even the Czech Prime Minister Alois Eliáš was among those arrested and was put on trial in Berlin. He was later spared from hanging but was kept hostage.

Although Heydrich would display public goodwill towards the populace of Bohemia and Moravia, his plan was to remove most of them to regions of Russian or murder them after the war had been won by Germany. Himmler told Heydrich that the overall vision for these lands was to see them annexed directly into the Reich, and those people that could not be Germanized would be exterminated.

On 10 October 1941, almost two weeks after Heydrich took control as Protector, he chaired a senior officer meeting in Prague of the RSHA outlining the 'Final Solution'. Their meeting was to discuss the fate of some 50,000 Jews in Bohemia and Moravia and plans of sending them all to the ghettos of Riga and Minsk. His officers also spoke about how to deal with the 5,000 Jews in Prague, but Heydrich had already proposed handing them directly over to his *Einsatzgruppen*. He made it clear in the meeting that he was now responsible for the implementation of transporting 60,000 Jews from Germany and Czechoslovakia to the Łódź Ghetto in Poland. He added that his responsibilities included establishing ghettos in the Protectorate as well. His position, he said, was enormous and vitally important. His main task now was to ensure that there was co-operation between his commanders and administrative leaders of various government departments in order for the implementation of the 'Final Solution' to the 'Jewish Question' in territories under German control.

Some weeks later Heydrich brought together these leaders to discuss the 'Final Solution'. This meeting was known as the Wannsee Conference and was held in Berlin in January 1942. The conference was to legalize the discrimination and removal of the Jewish race from existence in the occupied territories. Heydrich invited representatives from several government ministries including State Secretaries from the Foreign Office, the Justice, Interior and State ministries, and also representatives from the SS. Also present was *SS-Obersturmbannführer* Adolf Eichmann. Heydrich had tasked Eichmann with facilitating and managing the logistics involved in the mass deportation of Jews to the ghettos and extermination camps in Nazi-occupied Europe. It was Eichmann at the conference that collected information for Heydrich and prepared the minutes.

During the conference it was agreed that it would be the Jews in the General Government that would be dealt with first. In fact, preparations had already been undertaken and the Nazi leadership was under no illusion that it required great organizational skills to deal with an effective means of mass murder. Already a pool of experts had been drafted in to undertake this mammoth task. Eichmann told Heydrich that he was fully aware that the problems of transporting large numbers of Jews to Russia and liquidating them would be a logistical nightmare, especially when the war in Russia had not been won. It was agreed that it was more practical to transport German and other Jews to Poland and to kill them immediately rather than send them further east. It was therefore suggested that a series of extermination camps, unlike that of Auschwitz, was to be constructed in Poland and used primarily to transport those that were deemed unfit for work and were to be killed.

The preparation for the extermination of the Jews in Poland was planned at the Wannsee Conference. It was here in Berlin where a special organization, later named Operation REINHARD, was established.

Operation REINHARD was the code-name given to the systemic annihilation of the Polish Jews in the General Government and it would mark the beginning of the most deadly phase of the programme: the use of extermination camps. The SS and Police Leader of the district of Lublin, *SS-Oberstgruppenführer* Odilo Globocnik, was appointed the commander of the operation. Globocnik was a ruthless and fanatical SS officer who believed wholeheartedly in the Nazi vision. From his office he planned and gossiped with his associates about the future SS colonization of the East and the task of preparing the extermination of the Jews in the General Government.

In order to undertake such an action against the Jews, killing centres were to be utilized for Operation REINHARD. Globocnik set to work immediately and brought in people that had been assigned to the euthanasia programme that had knowledge and experience of setting up and operating factories for mass murder. Planning and the construction of three death camps were put forward, which included sites at Belzec, Sobibor and Treblinka. All three camps were to be unique as their purpose was different from other concentration camps. They were all to achieve their purpose by killing and using subterfuge and misdirection to conceal the truth by tricking their victims into co-operating.

As for Heydrich, he would not live to see the outcome of the operation. In May 1942 he would be attacked by Czech assassins and die of his injuries eight days later.

Konrad Meyer with leading Nazis including Heydrich during an exhibition on structure and planning in the East on 20 March 1941 in Berlin. Hitler's deputy Rudolf Hess can be seen here along with Reich Minister for Armament and Munitions, Fritz Todt.

A portrait of Heydrich.

(**Above**) Heydrich and Himmler's trip to Estonia in September 1941. Over the weeks to come, as German troops of Army Group North advanced through the Baltic states of Lithuania, Latvia and Estonia, *Einsatzgruppen* A followed in its wake, systematically rounding up Jews and murdering them. However, in spite of the mass killings, by November 1941 Himmler told Heydrich that he had become increasingly disgruntled by the slow pace at which the exterminations were taking place in the Baltics. Although action in Lithuania had proven successful, in Latvia the *Reichsführer* wanted to transport Jews from Germany into the area and then have them murdered.

(**Opposite, above**) A huge pile of personal belongings and dead Jews, murdered by members of the *Einsatzgruppen* A and Lithuanian auxiliaries, in the compound of Fort VII in Kovno, July 1941. In July alone more than 3,000 people were killed at this fort. At least 200 others were murdered at Fort V and 500 at Fort IV in this period. The anti-Jewish violence became more systematic after the German *Einsatzkommando* III, led by *SS-Standartenführer* Karl Jaeger, asserted control over the area towards the end of the summer. Heydrich considered this a great success and was eager to visit the killing grounds.

(**Opposite, below**) Heydrich is appointed Deputy Reich Protector of the Protectorate of Bohemia and Moravia on 27 September 1941. A day later he arrives at Prague Castle.

(**Above**) Heydrich takes the salute inside Prague Castle following his new appointment.

(**Opposite**) Two photographs taken in sequence showing Heydrich and *SS-Obergruppenführer* Karl Hermann Frank taking the salute in Prague. Frank had great power in the Protectorate. He controlled not only Nazi police apparatus in the Protectorate but the Gestapo, the SD and the *Kripo* as well.

Himmler is seen here at Prague Castle inspecting troops. Following closely behind is Heydrich.

Here Frank is shown standing to the right of Heydrich. When Heydrich was transferred to Prague, Nazi resistance was still quite strong. The Reich Protector was determined to make it his main mission to hunt down and murder every member of the Resistance. Heydrich's reign was often referred to by the Czechs as the 'Heydrich Terror'.

(**Above**) Heydrich, accompanied by the governor general of Poland, Karl Hermann Frank, climbing the entrance steps to the Castle of Prague in September 1941.

(**Opposite, above**) Heydrich speaking at the press conference for Czech journalists in Prague in September 1941.

(**Opposite, below**) Emil Dominik Josef Hácha hands a gift to Heydrich following his new appointment in Prague. After the *Anschluss* of March 1939, Hácha was the nominal State President of the newly-proclaimed German Protectorate of Bohemia and Moravia. However, Hácha was soon to lose all remaining influence over political affairs in his country when Heydrich took control and Hácha became a puppet. Many of his colleagues and friends were arrested, murdered or sent to concentration camps.

Hácha sits and discusses new policies with Heydrich in September 1941. Practically powerless, Hácha agreed to collaborate with Heydrich and had to watch while his country was terrorized by the Nazi regime. It was made worse by plans for the 'Final Solution in Prague', which disrupted the whole region and forced Hácha to collaborate. The Czech people regarded this as a betrayal.

Göring warmly shakes the hand of Heydrich. It was Göring who authorized Heydrich to coordinate resources of the Reich for a 'solution of the Jewish Question' throughout Europe.

Der Reichsmarschall des Großdeutschen Reiches
Beauftragter für den Vierjahresplan
Vorsitzender des Ministerrats für die Reichsverteidigung

Berlin, den . 7.1941

An den

Chef der Sicherheitspolizei und des SD
SS-Gruppenführer H e y d r i c h

B e r l i n.

Jn Ergänzung der Jhnen bereits mit Erlaß vom 24.I.39 übertragenen Aufgabe, die Judenfrage in Form der Auswanderung oder Evakuierung einer den Zeitverhältnissen entsprechend möglichst günstigsten Lösung zuzuführen, beauftrage ich Sie hiermit, alle erforderlichen Vorbereitungen in organisatorischer, sachlicher und materieller Hinsicht zu treffen für eine Gesamtlösung der Judenfrage im deutschen Einflußgebiet in Europa.

Soferne hierbei die Zuständigkeiten anderer Zentralinstanzen berührt werden, sind diese zu beteiligen.

Jch beauftrage Sie weiter, mir in Bälde einen Gesamtentwurf über die organisatorischen, sachlichen und materiellen Vorausmaßnahmen zur Durchführung der angestrebten Endlösung der Judenfrage vorzulegen.

Göring

A July 1941 letter from Göring to Heydrich outlining the 'Final Solution of the Jewish Question'. This letter gave written authorization to Heydrich and his senior group leaders to prepare and submit a plan for a 'total solution of the Jewish question' in territories under German control and to coordinate the participation of all involved government organizations.

The villa *Am Großen Wannsee* 56–58 where the Wannsee Conference was held. The purpose of the conference, ordered by the director of the Reich Security Main Office, was to ensure the co-operation of administrative leaders of various government departments in the implementation of the 'Final solution to the Jewish question'. The conference participants included representatives from several government ministries including State Secretaries from the Foreign Office, the Justice, Interior and State ministries, and representatives from the SS.

One of the key members at the Wannsee Conference was none other than *SS-Obersturmbannführer* Adolf Eichmann, who was one of the major organizers of the Holocaust, the 'Final Solution to the Jewish Question'. He was tasked with facilitating and managing the logistics involved in the mass deportation of Jews to ghettos and extermination camps in Nazi-occupied Eastern Europe. At Wannsee, Eichmann oversaw the stenographer who took the minutes and prepared the official distributed record of the meeting. It was agreed by Heydrich under Eichmann's supervision that he would organize large-scale deportations to extermination camps. These would eventually include Belzec, Sobibor and Treblinka, known as the 'Reinhard Camps'. The genocide would be code-named Operation REINHARD, this name being given in honour of Heydrich when he was assassinated in Prague a few months later.

Following the Wannsee Conference, Heydrich distributed orders across the occupied Eastern territories to commence preparations for the complete extermination of the Jews. Here in this photograph Jewish men are rounded up by German police for forced labour and escorted along Krakowskie Przedmiescie Street to a work site.

A group of Jewish men have been rounded up and their fate can only be imagined.

Widespread ad hoc executions across the Eastern territories still continued. In this photograph the last Jew to be executed is ordered to the edge of a grave pit.

Jews during a deportation action being sent to a concentration camp. At the Wannsee Conference Heydrich was aware of the problems of transporting large numbers of Jews to Russia and liquidating them. He came to the conclusion that it was more practical to transport German and other Jews to Poland and to kill them immediately rather than send them further east. As a result, he ordered a series of extermination camps, unlike that of Auschwitz, to be constructed in Poland and used primarily to transport those that were deemed unfit for work and were to be killed. The SS and Police Leader of the district of Lublin, *SS-Oberstgruppenführer* Odilo Globocnik, was appointed the commander of the operation. Specific deportation orders came from Heydrich's RSHA superior, Gestapo chief Müller, acting on Himmler's behalf. Eichmann's office was made responsible for collecting information on the Jews in each area, organizing the seizure of their property and arranging for and scheduling trains for deportations.

Chapter Four

Death and Retaliation

Following the occupation of the Czech lands by the Nazis, resistance was kept to a minimum and those that did rise in any type of opposition were immediately pacified. However, because of Heydrich's ruthlessness, total contempt for humanity and a combination of terror and hatred against the Czech people, the exiled government was determined that they had to do something that would inspire the Czechoslovakian people as well as demonstrate to senior Nazis controlling Bohemia and Moravia that they could still resist against the regime. It was decided that due to Heydrich's status, plans would be made to assassinate him.

The plan to kill Heydrich was put together by the Chief Czechoslovakian Intelligence Officer František Moravec, who coordinated the plan with the Special Operations Executive (SOE). The SOE was a secret British intelligence organization with the sole purpose of conducting espionage, sabotage and reconnaissance in occupied Europe. It was agreed that SOE-trained Czech assassins would be given the task of killing Heydrich by secretly being parachuted into Czechoslovakia. The operation was given the code-name ANTHROPOID, Greek for 'having the form of a human', a term normally used in zoology.

Training was undertaken in Scotland and supervised by the nominated head of the Czech section, Major Alfgar Hesketh-Prichard. Following initial delays in the planning and preparation of the operation, Jozef Gabčík and Jan Kubiš were selected to undertake the assassination.

On 28 December 1941, the ANTHROPOID pair landed near Nehvizdy, east of Prague and then made their way into the city to 'safe houses' to prepare for the attack. At first Gabčík and Kubiš planned to kill Heydrich on a train, but after assessment of the practicalities they realized that this was not going to be possible. They then decided to kill him on a forest road that led from Heydrich's home to Prague. However, this plan was called off and they agreed that it would be far easier and less dangerous for them to assassinate him during his commute into Prague.

His daily commute started from his home in Panenské Břežany, 9 miles north of central Prague, to his headquarters at Prague Castle. Gabčík and Kubiš waited at a tram stop at the junction between the road then known as Kirchmayerova třída and V Holešovičkách in Prague 8-Liben near Bulovka Hospital. The tight curve of the road meant that Heydrich's car, a green open-topped Mercedes 320 Cabriolet B, would have to slow down, and it would be here that they would attack him.

On the morning of 27 May 1942, as Heydrich's Mercedes slowed down and rounded the corner with no escort protection, Gabčík, who had concealed a Sten submachine gun under his raincoat, tried to shoot Heydrich but the gun jammed. As the car passed, Heydrich stood up and drew his Luger pistol, shouting at his driver *SS-Oberscharführer* Johannes Klein to stop the car. As the car began braking, Kubiš quickly threw a modified anti-tank grenade but misjudged the distance, with the bomb ending up exploding against the rear wheel. Although the attack appeared to have failed, the detonation severely wounded Heydrich, with splinters ripping through the right rear fender and embedding fragmentation and fibres from the upholstery of the car into Heydrich. There were serious injuries to his left side, including a puncture to his lung, spleen and diaphragm, as well as cracking of his ribs.

In the panic and confusion that ensued, Gabčík dropped his Sten gun and tried to flee the scene on his bicycle, but was forced to abandon this attempt and took cover behind a telegraph pole, firing at an injured Heydrich with his pistol. As Heydrich collapsed onto the pavement, Gabčík then ran from the scene with Klein in pursuit.

As Gabčík and Kubiš escaped from the scene, Heydrich was rushed to hospital, contorted with pain. He was immediately operated on, with the surgeons reinflating his collapsed left lung, suturing his torn diaphragm, inserting several catheters, removing the tip of his fractured eleventh rib and removing his spleen which contained fragments of a grenade and upholstery. Due to the severity of his injuries, Himmler sent his personal physician Karl Gebhardt to Prague; he cared for Heydrich and administered huge amounts of morphine to him.

Over the next few days Heydrich's recovery appeared to progress well, but on 3 June, while sitting up and having a midday meal, he suddenly collapsed and went into shock. His health then deteriorated and he soon slipped into a deep coma, never regaining consciousness. He died in the early hours of 4 June, with the doctor giving sepsis as the cause of death.

Hitler, enraged by Heydrich's assassination, ordered a investigation and reprisals, suggesting that Himmler send *SS-Obergruppenführer* Erich von dem Bach-Zelewski to Prague to mete out harsh retributions to what he considered were politically unreliable Czechs. The idea was justified in the eyes of a ruthless commander like Bach-Zelewski, but economically the Czech lands were regarded as an important industrial area for the German military and wholesale killings of the population could reduce the productivity of the region.

However, in spite of this some 13,000 people were arrested. A state of emergency was immediately proclaimed and a curfew was imposed in Prague. It was then announced that anyone who had helped the assassins was to be executed along with their families. This later included Jan Kubiš' girlfriend Anna Malinová, who was later to die in Mauthausen concentration camp. The village of Lidice was also implicated in the reprisals for Heydrich's death. Nazi intelligence misleadingly identified the village as a hiding-place of the assassins.

On 10 June 1942, just two days after an elaborate funeral was held for Heydrich in Prague, SS units committed what was known as the Lidice massacre. German troops marched into the village and killed 199 men and rounded up 195 women, deporting them to Ravensbrück concentration camp. All ninety-five children of Lidice were taken prisoner, with eighty-one later murdered in gas vans at the Chelmno concentration camp. The Czech village of Ležáky was also razed to the ground as Nazi intelligence said they had discovered a radio transmitter belonging to the SOE. All the men and women were murdered and both villages were set on fire, bombed and blasted, and the ruins of Lidice levelled and removed from the map.

On the day of the Lidice massacre a State funeral was held in Berlin for Heydrich. His coffin had been placed on a train from Prague and journeyed to the Reich capital. Himmler was waiting at the station for him to begin the procession through the sprawling Berlin streets to the Reich Chancellery to begin the service. Hitler was there at the Chancellery and he placed Heydrich's decorations, including the highest grade of the German Order, the Blood Order Medal, the Wound Medal, the Wound Badge in Gold and the War Merit Cross 1st Class with Swords on his funeral pillow. Heydrich was then transported on the back of a 10.5cm gun carriage and interred in Berlin's *Invalidenfriedhof* (Invalids' Cemetery) with Himmler taking the Nazi salute at his grave in his honour.

Following the State funeral of Heydrich, SD and Gestapo agents, following a massive manhunt, managed to track down Gabčík and Kubiš along with the assailants who had taken refuge in Prague's Cyril and Methodius Cathedral. On 18 June, over the course of a few hours the church was surrounded by 800 members of the SS and Gestapo under the command of *SS-Gruppenführer* Karl Fischer von Treuenfeld. What followed was a gunfight inside the church that saw a number of German troops killed plus several Czechs. The remainder hid in the church's crypt. The Germans then attempted to flush the men out with gunfire, tear gas and by flooding the crypt. Finally an entrance was made using explosives. However, rather than capitulate and face certain death by execution, Gabčík and Kubiš killed themselves. Supporters of the assassins who were killed following the fighting inside the church included the church's leader Bishop Gorazd, who is now revered as a martyr of the Orthodox Church.

Following the death of Heydrich, who had earned the nickname of 'Butcher of Prague', his assassination had not only spurred an orgy of revenge which resulted in the deaths of thousands of people, but also cowed the occupied country. In fact on 3 July 1942 some 200,000 Czechs were forced to gather on Wenceslas Square and were humiliated by being told to pledge their loyalty to the Reich and to give the Nazi salute. Although the Protector of Bohemia and Moravia was dead, the inhabitants of the city were to endure almost three years under Nazi rule which saw almost 80 per cent of the Slovak pre-war population die during this time. Heydrich's death came at a terrible cost and although it did not change the course of the war, the assassination's most important impact was psychological. The Nazi hierarchy would never feel safe again.

(**Above**) Unbeknown to Heydrich, in London the Czechoslovak government-in-exile planned to kill the Protectorate's leader. Jan Kubiš and Jozef Gabčík were chosen to undertake the assassination. They were trained by the British Special Operations Executive (SOE). Just three months after Heydrich moved to Prague, both SOE operatives were airlifted along with seven exiled soldiers from Czechoslovakia's army and two other groups named Silver A and Silver B (who had different missions) by an RAF Halifax of No. 138 Squadron into Czechoslovakia at 10.00pm on 28 December 1941. Under cover and in civilian dress, they walked to Prague where they had anti-Nazi contacts who helped them during the preparations for the assassination.

(**Opposite**) Heydrich, accompanied by his wife Lina, attending a concert at the opening of Prague's music week. The performance was held in the opulent setting of the Waldstein Palace with music by Richard Bruno, Heydrich's father. As the evening progressed Heydrich savoured his achievements and spoke to his wife about a bright future in the highest realms of the Nazi Party. However, he did not know that the next day, 27 May 1942, there were other plans unfolding for him.

The first of four photographs showing the damaged Mercedes following the attempted assassination of Heydrich. On the morning of 27 May 1942 he left his country mansion to drive to Prague airport. He was to fly to Berlin for an important meeting with Hitler. His briefcase was full of ambitious plans to destroy resistance to Nazi rule. Heydrich had no fear of physical attack. Being by nature an arrogant and self-righteous figure, he was openly contemptuous of the Czech people who, in his words, 'had no guts to do anything'. While leading Nazis, above all Hitler, travelled everywhere in armoured limousines with bulletproof glass and surrounded by bodyguards, Heydrich drove in the front seat of his open 3.5-litre Mercedes convertible. Despite orders issued at the beginning of May for the installation of armour-plating in the bodywork and seat plates of the Mercedes, nothing had been done, a mistake which was to cost Heydrich his life. Both assassins, Jan Kubiš and Jozef Gabčík, took advantage of Heydrich's lack of fear and planned to kill him at the tram stop on the curve of the road near Bulovka Hospital in Prague 8-Liben. As Heydrich's Mercedes SS-3 approached the corner of the road, both men waited as a tram passed and Heydrich's car slowed. Gabčík then dropped his raincoat concealing a British Sten gun, typically used by the SOE, and stepped into the road and pulled the trigger. Nothing happened. The gun had jammed. Gabčík was left standing helplessly. The Mercedes swept past, but Heydrich then made a fatal error. He stood up and drew his pistol, yelling at the driver to stop. Kubiš stepped from cover and threw his fused bomb that was hidden in a brown leather briefcase. In that moment the fate of Heydrich and thousands of others was sealed. As the driver took up chase, Heydrich slumped onto the bonnet, wounded by the explosion.

A Czech newspaper reports on the assassination of Heydrich and the declaration of martial law. As Heydrich lay in hospital wounded by the bomb explosion, drifting in and out of consciousness, a massive manhunt began in Prague. Some 21,000 police and SS searched more than 36,000 houses in the city. They found no trace of the attackers.

ATENTÁT

na Zastupujícího říšského protektora

Deset milionů K odměny

za předmětné údaje, které povedou k dopadení pachatelů

Dne 27. května 1942 asi v 10.30 hod. byl spáchán atentát na Zastupujícího říšského protektora SS-Obergruppenführera Heydricha. Zastupující říšský protektor přijížděl svým autem směrem z Panenských Břežan Kirchmayerovou třídou v městské čtvrti Praha-Libeň a chtěl zahnout do ulice V Holešovičkách, aby jel dále do města. Tu se postavil vozu v cestu muž, jenž se pokoušel vystřelit z automatické pistole na osoby sedící ve voze. Současně hodil druhý muž proti vozu třaskavinu, která při nárazu vybuchla. Po atentátu prchal jeden pachatel Kirchmayerovou třídou a ulicí Na Kolinské do ulice Na Zápalčí do řeznického obchodu Františka Braunera číslo domu 22. Odtud pak, když byl vypálil několik výstřelů, pokračoval v útěku v ulici Na Zápalčí k ulici V Holešovičkách, pravě směrem do města. Druhý pachatel uprchl na připraveném velocipedu Kirchmayerovou třídou směrem k městské čtvrti Stará Libeň.

Tento pachatel byl muž střední velikosti, štíhlý, měl na sobě tmavé až černé šaty a černý klobouk. Druhý pachatel, ten, který uprchl Kirchmayerovou třídou a ulicí Na Kolinské, je popisován takto: vysoký 160 až 162 cm, široký v ramenou, silná postava, plný, okrouhlý, sluncem opálený obličej, široká ústa s ohrnutými rty, tmavé dozadu sčesané vlasy; stáří asi 30—35 let. Tento muž měl na sobě tmavé až tmavohnědé šaty se světlými proužky a hnědé střevíce. Pokrývku hlavy při útěku neměl.

Jeden z pachatelů zanechal na místě činu světle, béžový plášť z balonového hedvábí, se světlými knoflíky. Každý z pachatelů měl tmavě hnědou aktovku, které byly nalezeny na místě činu. V jedné z těchto aktovek byla poloplačená balonová čepice béžové barvy z velbloudí srsti, na níž je velká okrouhlá modrobílá značka firmy obchodního domu „Bílá labuť". Pachatel, jenž uprchl pěšky, zanechal v blízkosti místa činu dámský velociped značky „Moto-Velo J. Krčmar, Teplice" tovární číslo 40.363. Tento dámský velociped má černé věnce kola (ráfy) s 9 mm širokými červenými pruhy, slonovinově červeně natřenou vidlice a rám, červeně černě lemovaná řidítka, červenohnědě dobře zachovalé pérované sedlo, hnědou torbu na nástroje, černé chránidlo řetězu a značně poškozenou tmavě až světle zbarvenou ochrannou síť. Na kole je poniklovaná hustilka s nežním držadlem a 25 cm dlouhou hadicí. Na tomto kole visela jedna z aktovek, nalezených na místě činu.

Pachatelé jistě čekali delší dobu, snad dokonce několik hodin na místě činu na Zastupujícího říšského protektora.

S poukazem na vypsanou odměnu 10,000.000 korun, která je stanovena na údaje z řad obyvatelstva, jež povedou k dopadení pachatelů a bude plně vyplacena, se předkládají tyto otázky:

1. Kdo může učiniti údaje o pachatelích?
2. Kdo pozoroval pachatele na místě činu?
3. Komu patří ony blíže popsané věci, obzvláště pak komu chybí onen popsaný dámský velociped, plášť, čepice a aktovky?

Tyto výše popsané věci jsou od dneška, od 9. hodiny vystaveny ve výkladní skříni obchodu s obuví Baťa, Praha II., Václavské nám. 6.

Kdo by mohl podati žádané informace, ale neučiní je z vlastní vůle policii, bude ve smyslu vyhlášeného nařízení říšského protektora v Čechách a na Moravě o vyhlášení civilního výjimečného stavu ze dne 27. května 1942 se svou rodinou zastřelen. Kromě toho je povinností všech majitelů domů, majitelů bytů a majitelů hotelů atd., počínaje dnem 28. května 1942, všechny policejně dosud nepřihlášené osoby v celém Protektorátě přihlásit s poukazem na toto vyhlášku příslušným policejním přihlašovacím úřadům. Provinilci proti tomuto nařízení se trestá smrtí.

Sdělení přijímá tajná státní policie, vedoucí úřadovna státní policie Praha, (Staatspolizeileitstelle Prag) v Praze II., Bredovská ulice čís. 20, čís. telefonu 30041, jakož i každý jiný německý nebo protektorátní policejní úřad, a to ústně, písemně nebo telefonicky.

Vyšší vedoucí SS a policie u říšského protektora v Čechách a na Moravě
podepsán: K. H. FRANK.

VÝNOS

říšského protektora v Čechách a na Moravě o vyhlášení civilního výjimečného stavu ze dne 27. května 1942.

V důsledku atentátu na Zastupujícího říšského protektora SS-Obergruppenführera Heydricha se ustanovuje toto:

Článek I.

jim poskytuje pomoc, anebo maje vědomost o jejich osobě nebo o jejich pobytu neučiní žádné oznámení, bude zastřelen se svou rodinou.

Článek III

As Heydrich's health deteriorated, Himmler flew his personal physician Dr Karl Gebhardt in to assume his care. Following a number of blood transfusions, Dr Theodor Morell, Hitler's personal physician, suggested to Gebhardt that he should treat Heydrich with sulfonamide, which was an early type of antibiotic. After a couple of days it appeared that Heydrich was slowly recovering from his injuries and Gebhardt refused Morell's advice, expecting that the patient would recover without antibiotic therapy. However, while sitting up in bed Heydrich went into shock and fell into a coma. He died of sepsis on 4 June 1942, eight days after the attack. Gebhardt's refusal to prescribe sulfonamide contributed to Heydrich's death. *(Bender)*

Seven photographs taken in sequence showing Heydrich's coffin being removed from the train in Berlin. Himmler can be seen accompanying the coffin along with SS leaders including Sepp Dietrich. Prior to the coffin being moved to Berlin, at midnight on 6 June the body was carried by torchlight up to Prague Castle from the hospital. The streets through which this ghostly procession passed were entirely cleared of civilians with thousands of SS men, police and Wehrmacht soldiers lining the route. On the morning of 7 June, Heydrich was laid in state in the castle courtyard. The coffin was guarded by senior SS officers and security police. Thousands of Czechs, terrified by possible retaliation, filed past in endless columns giving the Nazi salute. Huge throngs of Prague citizens lined the city's Wenceslas Square with the womenfolk wearing mourning clothes and carrying flowers. Early that evening the body was carried across the river beneath the saints and martyrs on the ancient Charles Bridge. The cortège wound its way along the cobbled streets to the main station where a special funeral train waited to take Heydrich on his last journey to Berlin. *(NA)*

Five photographs showing soldiers carrying the coffin out of the front entrance of the station to the 10.5cm gun carriage and loading it for the journey to the Reich Chancellery. Himmler can be seen in a couple of the photos, in one of which he is saluting. Note the first three images showing SS soldiers holding Heydrich's decorations, including the highest grade of the German Order, the Blood Order Medal, the Wound Medal, the Wound Badge in Gold and the War Merit Cross 1st Class with Swords on his funeral pillow. *(NA)*

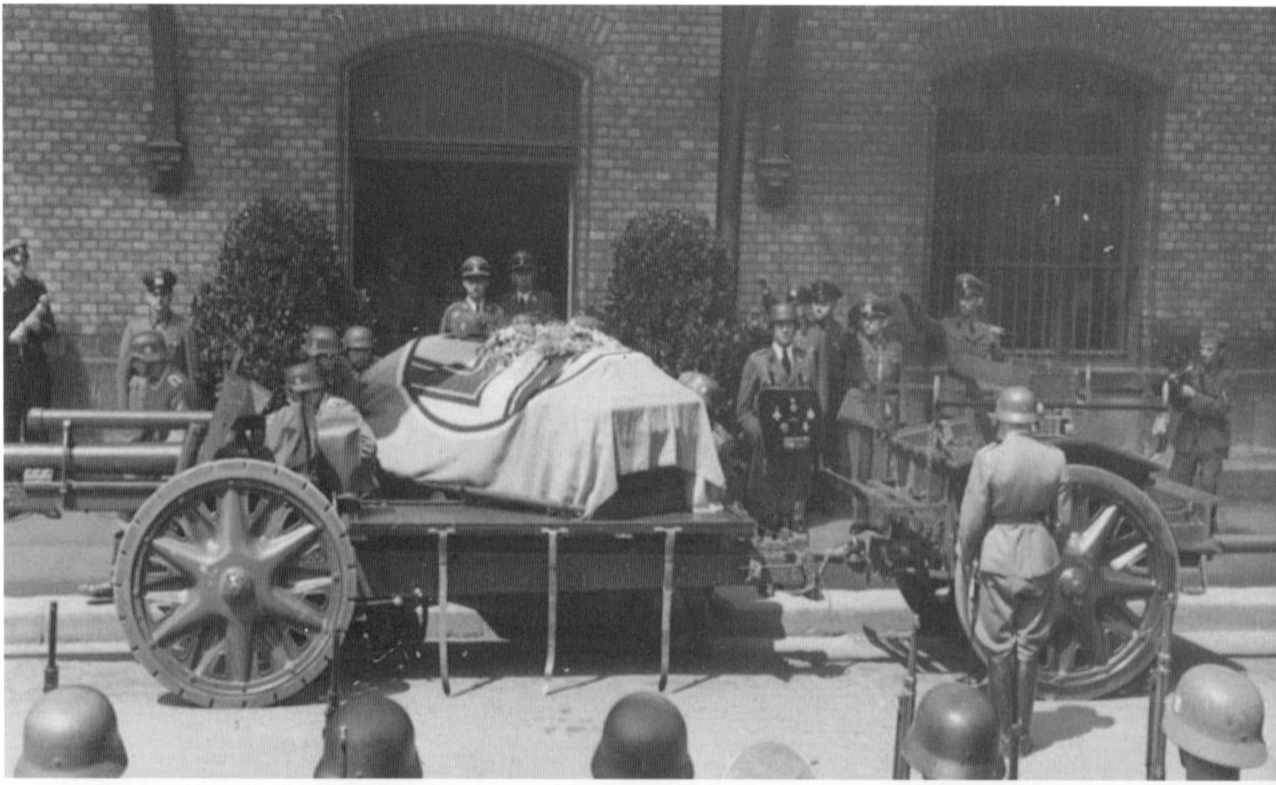

Berliners young and old line the streets in Berlin intermingled with Wehrmacht and SS soldiers, all trying to get a glimpse of Heydrich's coffin being hauled through the sprawling streets of the Reich capital. *(NA)*

Five photographs showing the funeral procession travelling from Berlin station to the Reich Chancellery. The coffin has been placed on the gun carriage of a 10.5cm artillery gun and towed by a prime mover. Thousands of people lined the roads for the State funeral. *(NA)*

engelhardt

Here the procession halts outside the Reich Chancellery. SS leaders and Nazi dignitaries are waiting outside before the coffin is removed from the gun carriage and carried into the Mosaic Hall to begin the service. Note a soldier detaching the coffin from the gun carriage in preparation for its removal. *(NA)*

SS soldiers carry the coffin from the gun carriage into the Reich Chancellery. (*NA*)

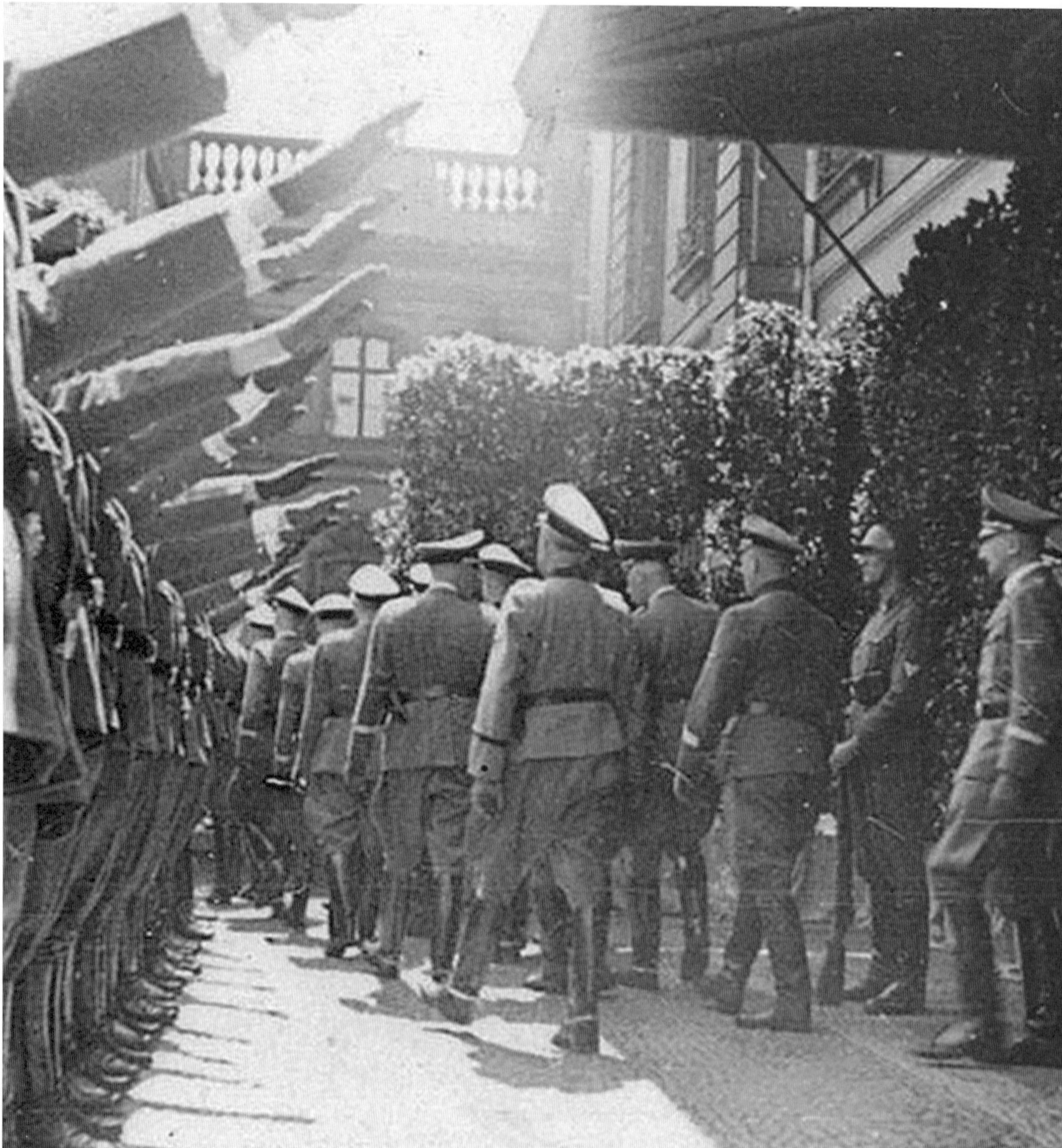

A photograph showing SS officers and Nazi leaders following the coffin into the Mosaic Hall. *(NA)*

Lit by torchlight, photographs show Heydrich's coffin in the Mosaic Hall surrounded by guards and leaders preparing for the ceremony.*(NA)*

The SS staged the most elaborate funeral ceremony ever held in the Third Reich. The chief mourner was Hitler. The event was attended by the most prominent leaders of the State and the army.(*NA*)

Hitler can be seen here entering the hall, saluting to his party leaders and dignitaries. Göring and Goebbels can also be seen present. Emil Hácha attended the funeral as well. *(NA)*

Hitler consoling the sons of Heydrich, Heider and Klaus, at the State funeral in Berlin. *(Bender)*

Hitler can be seen here meeting Heydrich's sons Klaus and Heider. *(Bender)*

Hitler salutes the coffin of his 'beloved Heydrich' before the ceremony commences. *(NA)*

Hitler can be seen here on the podium undertaking the eulogy to Heydrich. He said: 'I have only a few words. He was one of the best National Socialists, one of the strongest defenders of the German Reich idea, one of the biggest enemies of all the enemies of the Reich. He is a martyr. He died for the preservation and protection of the Reich. As leader of the party and as a leader of the German Reich, I award you, my dear comrade Heydrich, the highest award that I give you: the Supreme Stage of the Teutonic Order.' Hitler then salutes Heydrich and returns to his seat. *(NA)*

The podium just before Himmler gave his eulogy to Heydrich. To the side of the podium lays the coffin flanked by SS and Security Police. Himmler spoke at length about Heydrich and his life. 'My leader!' he said, 'dear Heydrich family! Honoured mourning guests! With the death of *SS-Obergruppenführer* Reinhard Heydrich, the Deputy Reich Protector of Bohemia and Moravia, Chief of the SD and Security Police, the National Socialist Movement has made a tragic sacrifice to the fight for freedom of our people. How incomprehensible to us is the thought that this shining, great human, scarcely 38 years old, is no longer with us and unable to battle along with his comrades. His unique abilities and pure character, his mind, his logic and clarity are irreplaceable. We would not be abiding by his wishes were we not here with his coffin, heroic thoughts of living and dying investing us, as they once did him.' He ended his speech by saying: 'On 27 May, an English bomb hit him from behind. A person paid from the ranks of the most worthless subhumans had surprised him. Fear and excessive caution were foreign to him, the greatest sportsman of the SS, a bold fencer, rider, pentathlon champion and swimmer. With courage and energy he defended himself and shot twice at his attackers, though he had been gravely wounded. For days we hoped that his hereditary strength and disciplined, healthy body would overcome his horrible injury. On the seventh day, 4 June 1942, destiny, God the almighty ancient, ended the life of Heydrich, a deep believer but the greatest opponent of the use of religion for political purposes. All of us, the kingdom's foremost leader that he served so loyally, are now gathered to honour Heydrich. He was at the time of his death a paragon of happy family life, and his two young sons are here to represent his courageous wife, who is expecting another child. Heydrich the leader is awarded the Gold Wound Badge and named, on the day of his death, a Waffen-SS unit on the Eastern Front, the 6th SS infantry, "Reinhard Heydrich". Heydrich wants to live on in our holy convictions, which were his words. He honoured and advanced the cause of those who shared his blood.' *(NA)*

Following the funeral service the coffin was then moved from the Reich Chancellery Mosaic Hall to be transported by horse-drawn gun carriage to Berlin's Invalidenfriedhof military cemetery. Here a column of SS, Security Police and Wehrmacht marches in front of the coffin. *(NA)*

Five photographs following the funeral service. In front of the Reich Chancellery the coffin draped in the Nazi national flag has been loaded onto the 10.5cm horse-drawn gun carriage and is being prepared to be transported through the streets of Berlin to the Invalidenfriedhof military cemetery. (*NA*)

Seven photographs showing Heydrich's coffin at Berlin's Invalidenfriedhof military cemetery. The name means 'Invalids' Cemetery' and it was named after a former veterans' hostel (*Invalidenhaus*) that used to be nearby (which also gave its name to the street Invalidenstraße). These photographs show mourners to be in section A, which abuts the north wall of the Invalidenfriedhof and Scharnhorststraße at the front of the cemetery. (*NA*)

DEUTSCHLAND
DEUTSCHLAND

The church of St Cyril and St Methodius in Resslova Street in Prague. This is where Kubiš and his group were found hiding on 18 June. Over the course of a few hours the church was surrounded by 800 members of the SS and Gestapo commanded by *SS-Gruppenführer* Karl Fischer von Treuenfeld. What followed was a gunfight inside the church which saw a number of German troops killed including several Czechs.

As the fighting inside the church intensified, the surviving assailants hid inside the crypt. In order to force them out, Karl Fischer ordered fire engine water hosepipes to be inserted into the bullet-scarred window of the church where Kubiš and his compatriots were cornered. Note in this photograph that more than one hosepipe was used to flush out those hiding inside. As the crypt filled with water, an entrance was made using explosives. However, rather than capitulate and face certain death by execution, Gabčík and Kubiš killed themselves.

A photograph of *SS-Gruppenführer* Karl Hermann Frank wearing RF-SS cuff titles indicating that he is personal staff of the *Reichsführer-SS*. It was Frank that was instrumental in initiating the destruction of the Czech villages of Lidice and Ležáky in order to take revenge on the Czech populace for Heydrich's death. *(Bender)*

On personal orders from Himmler the destruction of the village of Lidice was to be filmed and this was undertaken by Franz Treml, a collaborator with German Intelligence. This image shows the aftermath of the destruction. In reprisal for the assassination of Heydrich all 173 men from the village who were over 15 years of age were executed on 10 June 1942. A number of them can be seen murdered in this field.

Officers stand among the rubble of Lidice during the demolition of the town's ruins. The village was set on fire and the remains of the buildings destroyed with explosives. All the animals in the village including pets were shot as well. Himmler wanted every part of the village to disappear and this even included those buried in the town cemetery. The remains were dug up, looted for gold fillings and jewellery, and destroyed. A 100-strong German work party was then sent in to remove all visible remains of the village and re-route the stream running through it as well as the roads. They then covered the entire area of the village with topsoil and planted crops.

This image is a still from Franz Treml's film crew filming the destruction of Lidice. This film served as document No. 379 at the Nuremberg trials in 1946.

A commemorative stamp honouring a so-called Martyr of Germany. This stamp was issued on 28 May 1943, exactly one year and a day after the attack on Heydrich. It also exists in a much rarer form as a special issue miniature sheet containing one stamp, which was given to the 800 or so officials who had attended Heydrich's funeral.

Chapter Five

In Memory

Photographs taken by Michal Výborný who lives in the city of Prague

Recently taken, this image shows the bend in the road where Heydrich's car was attacked. It was at the junction between the road then known as Kirchmayerova třída and V Holešovičkách in Prague 8-Liben near Bulovka Hospital. The curve of the road meant that Heydrich's car would have to slow down and it would be here that the attack would take place. After so many years since 1942, the local geography has greatly changed. Kirchmayerova třída, now named Zenklova, no longer intersects V Holešovičkách. Although there is still a junction in the same place, it is formed by V Holešovičkách and two access ramps of the surrounding traffic interchange, the three roads together forming a triangular traffic island inside the hairpin turn where Kirchmayerova třída formerly intersected V Holešovičkách.

A monument at the place of the ambush on Heydrich. The figures are manufactured from bronze cast from a clay-modelled statue. The column is made of welded steel enclosed by Corten (weathered) steel. Because the memorial is located at a busy junction, it has been designed so that passing observers in their vehicles can clearly see the memorial and its proper scale.

The stone memorial to the attack on Heydrich. The steel memorial can clearly be seen near the road.

Three photographs of the Cathedral of Saints Cyril and Methodius in the centre of Prague's New Town. It was here that the SS stormed the building and an armed battle raged. After a fierce gun battle, two of the Czechoslovaks were killed and the rest committed suicide to avoid capture.

The bullet-scarred window of the crypt. This is where *SS-Gruppenführer* Fischer von Treuenfeld ordered that firemen's hoses be used to flush out the defenders hiding there.

An image showing the window of the crypt looking out. Note the dug-out brickwork and masonry at the bottom right. The defenders desperately began trying to dig an escape route out of the crypt, knowing there was no way out for them.

(**Above**) Here in the church's crypt is where Operation ANTHROPOID came to a violent end. The stairs were the entrance. Busts of Kubiš, Jozef Gabčík, Josef Bublík, Adolf Opálka, Josef Valčík, Jaroslav Švarc and Jan Hrubý are displayed here.

(**Opposite, above**) A view of the crypt inside the dimly-lit room where the busts of Jan Kubiš and Jozef Gabčík can be seen together with flowers and wreaths honouring their heroism. Almost everything is exactly as it was in 1942.

(**Opposite, below**) A bronze plaque in memory of the children of Lidice that were taken away from the village following its destruction and later murdered.

rotmistr pěchoty JAN KUBIŠ
* 24. 6. 1913 † 18. 6. 1942

82 DĚTÍ Z LIDIC ZAVRAŽDĚNÝCH PLYNEM NACISTY V ROCE 1942
NA PAMÁTKU MILIONŮ DĚTSKÝCH OBĚTÍ II. SVĚTOVÉ VÁLKY
82 CHILDREN OF LIDICE GASSED BY THE NAZIS IN 1942
IN MEMORY OF THE MILLIONS OF CHILDREN WHO PERISHED
IN THE SECOND WORLD WAR
82 KINDER AUS LIDICE, UMGEBRACHT DURCH VERGASUNG
VON DEN NAZIS IM JAHRE 1942
ZUM GEDENKEN AN DIE MILLIONEN KINDER, DIE DEM II. WELTKRIEG
ZUM OPFER GEFALLEN SIND

A cross at the Lidice Memorial in memory of the village people that were murdered.

Two photographs showing sprawling fields where Lidice once stood. The village was completely decimated and the remains buried. Himmler wanted the place completely removed from the map.

The Lidice Memorial stands as a grim reminder of the horrors endured by the people of the village.

The bronze statue of the children of Lidice. Some 173 men from the village were shot in the garden of the Horak farm. The women and children were taken to the gymnasium of Kładno grammar school. Three days later the children were taken from their mothers and, except for those selected for re-education in German families and those less than a year old, were murdered in gas vans at Chelmno concentration camp. The women of the village were sent to Ravensbrück concentration camp and died.

Appendix I

Order from Hermann Göring to Reinhard Heydrich

Berlin, 31 July 1941

To *Gruppenführer* Heydrich:

Supplementing the task assigned to you by the decree of 24 January 1939, to solve the Jewish problem by means of emigration and evacuation in the best possible way according to present conditions, I hereby charge you to carry out preparations as regards organizational, financial and material matters for a total solution (*Gesamtlösung*) of the Jewish question in all the territories of Europe under German occupation.

Where the competency of other central organizations touches on this matter, these organizations are to collaborate.

I charge you further to submit to me as soon as possible a general plan of the administrative material and financial measures necessary for carrying out the desired final solution (Endlösung) of the Jewish question.

Göring

Appendix II

Wannsee Conference Minutes

Headed by *SS-Obergruppenführer* Heydrich

I.

The following persons took part in the discussion about the final solution of the Jewish question which took place in Berlin, at Grossen Wannsee No. 56/58 on 20 January 1942:

Gauleiter Dr. Meyer and *Reichsamtleiter* Dr. Leibbrandt	Reich Ministry for the Occupied Eastern territories
Secretary of State Dr. Stuckart	Reich Ministry for the Interior
Secretary of State Neumann	Plenipotentiary for the Four-Year Plan
Secretary of State Dr. Freisler	Reich Ministry of Justice
Secretary of State Dr. Bühler	Office of the Government General
Under Secretary of State Dr. Luther	Foreign Office
SS-Oberführer Klopfer	Party Chancellery
Ministerialdirektor Kritzinger	Reich Chancellery
SS-Gruppenführer Hofmann	Race and Settlement Main Office
SS-Gruppenführer Müller and *SS-Obersturmbannführer* Eichmann	Reich Main Security Office
SS-Oberführer Dr. Schongarth Commander of the Security Police and the SD in the Government General	Security Police and SD
SS-Sturmbannführer Dr. Lange Commander of the Security Police and the SD for the General-District Latvia, as deputy of the Commander of the Security Police and the SD for the Reich Commissariat 'Eastland'	Security Police and SD

II.

At the beginning of the discussion Chief of the Security Police and of the SD, *SS-Obergruppenführer* Heydrich, reported that the Reich Marshal had appointed him delegate for the preparations for the final solution of the Jewish question in Europe and pointed out that this discussion had been called for the purpose of clarifying fundamental questions. The wish of the Reich Marshal to have a draft sent to him concerning organizational, factual and material interests in relation to the final solution of the Jewish question in Europe makes necessary an initial common action of all central offices immediately concerned with these questions in order to bring their general activities into line.

The *Reichsführer-SS* and the Chief of the German Police (Chief of the Security Police and the SD) was entrusted with the official central handling of the final solution of the Jewish question without regard to geographic borders.

The Chief of the Security Police and the SD then gave a short report of the struggle which has been carried on thus far against this enemy, the essential points being the following:

a) the expulsion of the Jews from every sphere of life of the German people,
b) the expulsion of the Jews from the living space of the German people.

In carrying out these efforts, an increased and planned acceleration of the emigration of the Jews from Reich territory was started, as the only possible present solution.

By order of the Reich Marshal, a Reich Central Office for Jewish Emigration was set up in January 1939 and the Chief of the Security Police and SD was entrusted with the management. Its most important tasks were

a) to make all necessary arrangements for the preparation for an increased emigration of the Jews,
b) to direct the flow of emigration,
c) to speed the procedure of emigration in each individual case.

The aim of all this was to cleanse German living space of Jews in a legal manner.

All the offices realized the drawbacks of such enforced accelerated emigration. For the time being they had, however, tolerated it on account of the lack of other possible solutions of the problem.

The work concerned with emigration was, later on, not only a German problem, but also a problem with which the authorities of the countries to which the flow of emigrants was being directed would have to deal. Financial difficulties, such as the demand by various foreign governments for increasing sums of money to be presented at the time of the landing, the lack of shipping space, increasing restriction of entry permits, or the cancelling of such, increased extraordinarily the difficulties of emigration. In spite of these difficulties, 537,000 Jews were sent out of the country between the takeover of power and the deadline of 31 October 1941. Of these

- approximately 360,000 were in Germany proper on 30 January 1933
- approximately 147,000 were in Austria (Ostmark) on 15 March 1939
- approximately 30,000 were in the Protectorate of Bohemia and Moravia on 15 March 1939.

The Jews themselves, or their Jewish political organizations, financed the emigration. In order to avoid impoverished Jews remaining behind, the principle was followed that wealthy Jews have to finance the emigration of poor Jews; this was arranged by imposing a suitable tax, i.e. an emigration tax, which was used for financial arrangements in connection with the emigration of poor Jews and was imposed according to income.

Apart from the necessary Reichsmark exchange, foreign currency had to be presented at the time of landing. In order to save foreign exchange held by Germany, the foreign Jewish financial organizations were – with the help of Jewish organizations in Germany – made responsible for arranging an adequate amount of foreign currency. Up to 30 October 1941, these foreign Jews donated a total of around 9,500,000 dollars.

In the meantime the *Reichsführer-SS* and Chief of the German Police had prohibited emigration of Jews due to the dangers of an emigration in wartime and due to the possibilities of the East.

III.

Another possible solution of the problem has now taken the place of emigration, i.e. the evacuation of the Jews to the East, provided that the Führer gives the appropriate approval in advance.

These actions are, however, only to be considered provisional, but practical experience is already being collected which is of the greatest importance in relation to the future final solution of the Jewish question.

Approximately 11 million Jews will be involved in the final solution of the European Jewish question, distributed as follows among the individual countries:

Country	*Number*
A. Germany proper	131,800
Austria	43,700
Eastern territories	420,000
General Government	2,284,000
Bialystok	400,000
Protectorate Bohemia and Moravia	74,200
Estonia – free of Jews	–

	Latvia	3,500
	Lithuania	34,000
	Belgium	43,000
	Denmark	5,600
	France/occupied territory	165,000
	unoccupied territory	700,000
	Greece	69,600
	Netherlands	160,800
	Norway	1,300
B.	Bulgaria	48,000
	England	330,000
	Finland	2,300
	Ireland	4,000
	Italy including Sardinia	58,000
	Albania	200
	Croatia	40,000
	Portugal	3,000
	Rumania incl. Bessarabia	342,000
	Sweden	8,000
	Switzerland	18,000
	Serbia	10,000
	Slovakia	88,000
	Spain	6,000
	Turkey (European portion)	55,500
	Hungary	742,800
	USSR	5,000,000
	Ukraine	2,994,684
	White Russia excluding Bialystok	446,484
	Total: over 11,000,000	

The number of Jews given here for foreign countries includes, however, only those Jews who still adhere to the Jewish faith, since some countries still do not have a definition of the term 'Jew' according to racial principles.

The handling of the problem in the individual countries will meet with difficulties due to the attitude and outlook of the people there, especially in Hungary and Rumania. Thus, for example, even today the Jew can buy documents in Rumania that will officially prove his foreign citizenship.

The influence of the Jews in all walks of life in the USSR is well known. Approximately 5 million Jews live in the European part of the USSR, in the Asian part scarcely

0.25 million. The breakdown of Jews residing in the European part of the USSR according to trades was approximately as follows:

Agriculture	9.1%
Urban workers	14.8%
In trade	20.0%
Employed by the state	23.4%
In private occupations such as medical	32.7%
profession, press, theatre, etc.	32.7%

Under proper guidance, in the course of the final solution the Jews are to be allocated for appropriate labour in the East. Able-bodied Jews, separated according to sex, will be taken in large work columns to these areas for work on roads, in the course of which action doubtless a large portion will be eliminated by natural causes.

The possible final remnant will, since it will undoubtedly consist of the most resistant portion, have to be treated accordingly, because it is the product of natural selection and would, if released, act as the seed of a new Jewish revival (see the experience of history).

In the course of the practical execution of the final solution, Europe will be combed through from west to east. Germany proper, including the Protectorate of Bohemia and Moravia, will have to be handled first due to the housing problem and additional social and political necessities.

The evacuated Jews will first be sent, group by group, to so-called transit ghettos, from which they will be transported to the East.

SS-Obergruppenführer Heydrich went on to say that an important prerequisite for the evacuation as such is the exact definition of the persons involved.

It is not intended to evacuate Jews over 65 years old, but to send them to an old-age ghetto – Theresienstadt is being considered for this purpose.

In addition to these age groups – of the approximately 280,000 Jews in Germany proper and Austria on 31 October 1941, approximately 30% are over 65 years old – severely wounded veterans and Jews with war decorations (Iron Cross I) will be accepted in the old-age ghettos. With this expedient solution, in one fell swoop many interventions will be prevented.

The beginning of the individual larger evacuation actions will largely depend on military developments. Regarding the handling of the final solution in those European countries occupied and influenced by us, it was proposed that the appropriate expert of the Foreign Office discuss the matter with the responsible official of the Security Police and SD.

In Slovakia and Croatia the matter is no longer so difficult, since the most substantial problems in this respect have already been brought near a solution. In Rumania the government has in the meantime also appointed a commissioner for

Jewish affairs. In order to settle the question in Hungary, it will soon be necessary to force an adviser for Jewish questions onto the Hungarian government.

With regard to taking up preparations for dealing with the problem in Italy, *SS-Obergruppenführer* Heydrich considers it opportune to contact the chief of police with a view to these problems.

In occupied and unoccupied France, the registration of Jews for evacuation will in all probability proceed without great difficulty.

Under Secretary of State Luther calls attention in this matter to the fact that in some countries, such as the Scandinavian states, difficulties will arise if this problem is dealt with thoroughly and that it will therefore be advisable to defer actions in these countries. Besides, in view of the small numbers of Jews affected, this deferral will not cause any substantial limitation.

The Foreign Office sees no great difficulties for south-east and western Europe.

SS-Gruppenführer Hofmann plans to send an expert to Hungary from the Race and Settlement Main Office for general orientation at the time when the Chief of the Security Police and SD takes up the matter there. It was decided to assign this expert from the Race and Settlement Main Office, who will not work actively, as an assistant to the police attaché.

IV.

In the course of the final solution plans, the Nuremberg Laws should provide a certain foundation, in which a prerequisite for the absolute solution of the problem is also the solution to the problem of mixed marriages and persons of mixed blood.

The Chief of the Security Police and the SD discusses the following points, at first theoretically, in regard to a letter from the chief of the Reich chancellery:

1) Treatment of Persons of Mixed Blood of the First Degree:
Persons of mixed blood of the first degree will, as regards the final solution of the Jewish question, be treated as Jews.

From this treatment the following exceptions will be made:

a) Persons of mixed blood of the first degree married to persons of German blood if their marriage has resulted in children (persons of mixed blood of the second degree). These persons of mixed blood of the second degree are to be treated essentially as Germans.
b) Persons of mixed blood of the first degree, for whom the highest offices of the Party and State have already issued exemption permits in any sphere of life. Each individual case must be examined, and it is not ruled out that the decision may be made to the detriment of the person of mixed blood.

The prerequisite for any exemption must always be the personal merit of the person of mixed blood (not the merit of the parent or spouse of German blood).

Persons of mixed blood of the first degree who are exempted from evacuation will be sterilized in order to prevent any offspring and to eliminate the problem of persons of mixed blood once and for all. Such sterilization will be voluntary. But it is required to remain in the Reich. The sterilized 'person of mixed blood' is thereafter free of all restrictions to which he was previously subjected.

2) Treatment of Persons of Mixed Blood of the Second Degree:
Persons of mixed blood of the second degree will be treated fundamentally as persons of German blood, with the exception of the following cases, in which the persons of mixed blood of the second degree will be considered as Jews:

a) The person of mixed blood of the second degree was born of a marriage in which both parents are persons of mixed blood.
b) The person of mixed blood of the second degree has a racially especially undesirable appearance that marks him outwardly as a Jew.
c) The person of mixed blood of the second degree has a particularly bad police and political record that shows that he feels and behaves like a Jew.

Also in these cases exemptions should not be made if the person of mixed blood of the second degree has married a person of German blood.

3) Marriages between Full Jews and Persons of German Blood:
Here it must be decided from case to case whether the Jewish partner will be evacuated or whether, with regard to the effects of such a step on the German relatives [this mixed marriage] should be sent to an old-age ghetto.

4) Marriages between Persons of Mixed Blood of the First Degree and Persons of German Blood:

a) Without Children:
If no children have resulted from the marriage, the person of mixed blood of the first degree will be evacuated or sent to an old-age ghetto (same treatment as in the case of marriages between full Jews and persons of German blood, point 3).
b) With Children:
If children have resulted from the marriage (persons of mixed blood of the second degree), they will, if they are to be treated as Jews, be evacuated or sent to a ghetto along with the parent of mixed blood of the first degree. If these children are to be treated as Germans (regular cases), they are exempted from evacuation as is the parent of mixed blood of the first degree.

5) Marriages between Persons of Mixed Blood of the First Degree and Persons of Mixed Blood of the First Degree or Jews.

In these marriages (including the children) all members of the family will be treated as Jews and therefore be evacuated or sent to an old-age ghetto.

6) Marriages between Persons of Mixed Blood of the First Degree and Persons of Mixed Blood of the Second Degree.

In these marriages both partners will be evacuated or sent to an old-age ghetto without consideration of whether the marriage has produced children, since possible children will as a rule have stronger Jewish blood than the Jewish person of mixed blood of the second degree.

SS-Gruppenführer Hofmann advocates the opinion that sterilization will have to be widely used, since the person of mixed blood who is given the choice whether he will be evacuated or sterilized would rather undergo sterilization.

State Secretary Dr. Stuckart maintains that carrying out in practice of the just mentioned possibilities for solving the problem of mixed marriages and persons of mixed blood will create endless administrative work. In the second place, as the biological facts cannot be disregarded in any case, State Secretary Dr. Stuckart proposed proceeding to forced sterilization.

Furthermore, to simplify the problem of mixed marriages possibilities must be considered with the goal of the legislator saying something like: 'These marriages have been dissolved.'

With regard to the issue of the effect of the evacuation of Jews on the economy, State Secretary Neumann stated that Jews who are working in industries vital to the war effort, provided that no replacements are available, cannot be evacuated.

SS-Obergruppenführer Heydrich indicated that these Jews would not be evacuated according to the rules he had approved for carrying out the evacuations then under way.

State Secretary Dr. Bühler stated that the General Government would welcome it if the final solution of this problem could be begun in the General Government, since on the one hand transportation does not play such a large role here nor would problems of labour supply hamper this action. Jews must be removed from the territory of the General Government as quickly as possible, since it is especially here that the Jew as an epidemic carrier represents an extreme danger and on the other hand he is causing permanent chaos in the economic structure of the country through continued black market dealings. Moreover, of the approximately 2.5 million Jews concerned, the majority is unfit for work.

State Secretary Dr. Bühler stated further that the solution to the Jewish question in the General Government is the responsibility of the Chief of the Security Police and the SD and that his efforts would be supported by the officials of the General Government. He had only one request: to solve the Jewish question in this area as quickly as possible.

In conclusion the different types of possible solutions were discussed, during which discussion both *Gauleiter* Dr. Meyer and State Secretary Dr. Bühler took the position that certain preparatory activities for the final solution should be carried out immediately in the territories in question, in which process alarming the populace must be avoided.

The meeting was closed with the request of the Chief of the Security Police and the SD to the participants that they afford him appropriate support during the carrying out of the tasks involved in the solution.

Notes

Notes

Notes

Notes

Notes